We Need the Sun

Heather Hammonds

Contents

The Sun	2
Daytime	4
Spring and Summer	6
Autumn and Winter	8
Plants and the Sun	10
Very Hot Places	12
Nighttime	14
Glossary	16

The Sun

The sun is like
a big, hot ball.
Light from the sun
shines on Earth.
We live on Earth.

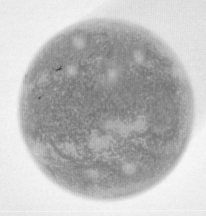

The sun warms Earth.
Warm sunshine helps plants
and animals to live.

Daytime

The sun comes up
in the morning.
It lights up the sky.
It is **sunrise**.

Many animals wake up.
We wake up, too.
It is daytime
when the sun is up.

Spring and Summer

In spring and summer,
there are lots of sunny days.
The sky is blue.
The sun warms the sea
and the land.

Some days are very hot.
We stay out of the sun
on hot days.

It is dangerous
to look at the sun.

Autumn and Winter

In autumn and winter,
it is not as sunny.
There are lots
of cloudy days.

It is cold in autumn
and winter.
It can rain or snow.

Plants and the Sun

Plants need sunshine
to help them grow.

The flowers in this garden
are growing fast
in the sunshine.

Very Hot Places

In some places,
it is very hot and sunny
all the time.

The sun shines every day.
It does not rain or snow.

Nighttime

The sun goes down
at the end of the day.
Sometimes the sky looks
red or orange.
It is **sunset**.

It is nighttime
when the sun has gone down.
The sun will come up again
tomorrow!

Glossary

Earth

sunrise

sunset